TEENAGE TAPESTRIES

THE REALITY AROUND YOU

ADIBA H. HUSSAIN

Writer's Pocket

First published by Writer's Pocket in 2024

email:editor@writerspocket.com

cover design by Adiba H. Hussain

ISBN-13: 978-93-6083-199-8

www.writerspocket.com

ABOUT THE AUTHOR

Adiba H. Hussain is a 14-year-old high-schooler. A girl with passion and enthusiasm for being a successful writer. She aims to achieve something more than what she dreamt of. An Indian writer, on her journey of discovering beautiful myths and facts,some scientific, some relating to stories widely spread among teens and young adults, and tracing them down on papers like the art of calligraphy.

Hey there, fellow book lovers! I'm Adiba H. Hussain, just a ninth-grader trying to juggle equations and metaphors. As you flip through this anthology, I hope my words leave a little sparkle in your day.

So, here's a bit about me—I'm your typical science student, curious about the universe and all its wonders. But when it comes to writing, that's where my heart truly lies. I'm still figuring out my future (aren't we all?), but one thing's for sure: my love for crafting stories is here to stay.

I remember a time when words felt like strangers, but then the world slowed down,and I found solace in the pages of books and the comfort of poetry. It was during those quiet days that I discovered my voice and the power it held.

Now, I'm on a mission to fill shelves with books that have my name on the spine. And guess what? You're a part of this dream. Your support, your feedback, it meansthe world to me. It's what keeps me writing, dreaming, and reaching for the stars.

I can't wait to hear from you, to learn what you think, and to share this journey withyou. So, let's chat, connect, and maybe even become friends.

You can reach out to me at:
E-mail- adiba.h.hussain.05.20@gmail.com
Instagram ID- @reality.xx.glow

Thanks for being here, for reading, and for inspiring me to keep going. Let's makesome magic with words, shall we?

With Love,
Adiba H. Hussain

For the restless hearts and curious minds,

This book is a tribute to the spirit of youth that forever binds.

Adiba, You wanted this to be done, right?
Here you are!
This book is for your past, present, and future self

CONTENTS

ACKNOWLEDGMENTS

Hii, I share my gratitude to all and one who have helped me through, even if their contribution was little.

I convey my thanks and loads of love to my AMMA and PAPA. Thank you for being there with me from the start till the end. Thank you so much Papa for helping me out with the publishing process. Here, I would like to give this big thanks to Amma, for listening to every page, from the first to the last, with her whole attention and praising me, making me content. Hehe. Thank you so much, I love you both a lot.

One more and really important person, Sudakhina, someone really close to me, I am grateful to you for all the possible support that you provided. Thank you for helping me with all the things that I did and went through. Thank you so much My Sunflower.

I would like to extend my gratitude to this dear friend of mine, Aleeza. Girl, you've helped me a lot with it. And I will never forget all your help and support. You guided me with tons of things and I am grateful to you for that. Thank you a lot Sistaa :)

Now, my little brother. Humaid, you don't have an idea of how much you have inspired me to work on this anthology. Handling you in one hand and writing from the other was a challenging task but an interesting one. To be honest, you are that shining star who did throw the light of happiness on my way. Thank you for helping me with this.

To my friends, my munchkins, Diksha, Palak, Siddhi, Sanvi, Tamazzur, and Niharika thank you so much for believing in me throughout the process, [I better say that I made you'll do that], I need to thank you all though.

To My Dear Cousin, thank you so much Asdaqa Di, for helping me out with some of my teenage spirals and being by my side throughout.

To my English teacher who taught me in 8th grade, Navjot Ma'am, I am grateful to be your student. You've guided me and taught me several things that I do and will always cherish.
Thank You ma'am for being the support that I was longing for.

To my Hindi teacher who taught me in 7th and 8th grade, Arunima Ma'am, I am honored to have a guide and a teacher like you. Thank you for all the morals you have taught me. I am going to remember all your lessons and guides.

To my English teacher in grade 3 and History teacher in grades 7 and 8, Anamika Ma'am, Thank you so much for teaching me all those English and Moralistic lessons that marked a base for me to grow on. Thank you for always appreciating and motivating me to move ahead.

To all the ones who have read this book or are reading it, I am boundlessly happy for your support. You've bought it and gone through the pages, what else can be a bigger gift than this? To all the ones who have supported me in this journey, whether being a reader or a partner in work, I am grateful to each one.

Wishing All of You Good Luck with What Ever You've Planned for Yourself! Loads Of Love <3

Reagrds,
Adiba H. Hussain

Writer's Note

I humbly present this anthology as a tribute to all the teenagers out there, as well as to my future self. When I am old and gray, I want to revisit these pages and bask in the same emotions and sensations that I feel now, during my teenage years.

Moreover, I implore both adults and young adults to peruse these passages and relive their teenage days, soak in the moments they may have missed out on, and be transported back to the dreamy land of their youth. It is my ardent hope that this anthology will serve as a time capsule, a reminder of the joys and tribulations of adolescence that we all experience at some point in our lives.

So go ahead, immerse yourself in the pages of this book, and allow yourself to feel all the feelings that come with being a teenager. Happy reading, and may you find solace and comfort in these words.

To the spirited voices of youth,
Whose thoughts, like stars, guide us through the night,
This anthology is dedicated to you,
The dreamers, the seekers, the light.

May these pages resonate with your heartbeats,
Echo your laughter, and reflect your tears,
For, within these stories, you'll find
The essence of teenage years.

To all who remember the bittersweet taste
Of adolescence, its trials, and its grace,
May you find within a familiar trace
Of your own journey through time and space.

So, to teens, adults, and young at heart,
Dive into this collection, and let the voyage start.

POETRIES

Echoes of Nurturing

Let us take the first step towards our youth. Here, the poetries are referred to the stage when we step into teenage life leaving our childhood behind. A moment to relax our minds and think about the blessings we have, close our eyes, and revise the memories we shared with our parents and surroundings.

Surrounded by the laughter of family and the comfort of home, we find the strength to journey through life's dance, hand in hand, step by step.

1. Mother's Perfume

A mother's perfume, oh what a scent,
It brings back memories of time well spent.
Those childhood hugs and bedtime stories,
Even the gentle kisses and sweet lullabies.

It's a scent that lingers in the air,
A fragrance of love beyond compare.
A mother's perfume, so sweet and pure,
A scent that will forever endure.

It's a signature scent that's uniquely hers,
A fragrance that no one else prefers.
It's a scent that takes us back in time,
To moments of love so pure and divine.

A mother's perfume, a comforting smell,
A scent that no words can truly tell.
It reminds us of love that's unconditional,
A bond that's forever unbreakable.

So let's cherish the scent of our mother's perfume,
And let it fill our hearts and rooms.
For it's a reminder of a love so true,
A love that will always stay with you.

2. A Father's Unyielding Love

A father's love is like a guiding light,
Always shining bright, even in the darkest night.
He teaches us to walk and then to run,
And always supports us until the job is done.

He shows us how to be strong and steady,
And to never give up, even when things get heavy.
His wisdom and kindness are gifts we treasure,
And his love for us is beyond all measure.

A father's embrace is a warm and safe place,
A reminder that no matter what, we will always have his grace.
We are grateful for the sacrifices he has made,
And for the love that will never fade.

So here's to all the fathers who have shown us the way,
We honor their strength, their love, and their unwavering sway.
Thank you for all that you do,
We celebrate and cherish you!

3. My Mister Sister

This is to my sister,
Who acts like a mischievous mister.
All girly girly in front of me,
And a tomboy, oh! She has to be.

Her love and care towards me shows her endearment,
On the other hand, her waves of rage and power are stronger than cement.
I may break into laughter cause she's funny,
But no wonder, being with her sometimes does make me feel uncanny.

To all the little siblings,
I know fighting and struggling is what we all do,
But elder ones are there as our moldings,
And these feelings are nothing out of the blue.

My Sister Mister is nothing so cool,
But she's hot-headed like fire on the coal.
Hunny Bunny, she doesn't want to have one,
But she loves Bunny's Bun.

4. Whispers Of A Brother's Love

Oh, dear sister, my heart aches to see
The pain and sorrow that's taken over thee
I know not the reason for your tears
But I'm here for you, to calm your fears

You've always been there for me, my guide
With love and patience, by my side
Now it's my turn to be strong for you
To offer comfort and help you through

Let me be the light in your darkest hour
To lift you up and give you power
Together we'll face the trials of life
And emerge stronger from the strife

Dear sister, don't despair or lose hope
For in your heart, there's a boundless scope
Of love, strength and resilience so true
And I'm here to remind you, I love you.

5. Echoes Across the Fence

In houses close, where windows meet,
Neighbors dwell, with stories sweet,
Each door is a portal to a life unknown,
In this mosaic of lives, seeds are sown.

From morning's light to evening's calm,
Neighbors share in joy and qualm,
A smile exchanged, a nod of care,
In this shared space, a bond to bear.

In gardens blooming, laughter rings,
As children play with boundless wings,
Their laughter, like a melody bright,
Binding hearts in the soft twilight.

Through open windows, voices flow,
In laughter, sorrow, high and low,
A symphony of daily life's embrace,
In this neighborhood's gentle grace.

In times of need, they lend a hand,
In unity, they firmly stand,
For neighbors know, in times of strife,
Together, they'll weave the thread of life.

In whispered secrets, friendships grow,
In shared moments, love does show,
For in these walls, more than bricks and stone,
Lies a community, where hearts are known.

So here's to neighbors, near and far,
In every corner, where shadows spar,
For in their presence, we find our kin,
In this tapestry of life, where love begins.

6. Petals of Souls

Flowers and people, much alike they seem,
Both so beautiful, both so unique in their dream.
Both have a story, both have a tale,
Both have a journey, both have a trail.

Flowers bloom and people grow,
Both have a purpose, both have a glow.
Both are delicate, both need care,
Both need love to fully share.

Flowers come in every shape and hue,
Just like people, each one is new.
Some are bold, some are shy,
Some are vibrant, some are sly.

People too, come in every shade,
Each one unique, each one handmade.
Some are outgoing, some are reserved,
Some are carefree, some are unnerved.

Flowers and people, both have a heart,
Both play a role, both have a part.
Both have emotions, both can feel,
Both can love, and both can heal.

So let's cherish both, flowers and people alike,
For they bring beauty to our life.
Let's learn from them, let's take a cue,
In how we can grow and bloom anew.

7. Power Of Our Surrounding

Blessed are they who see beautiful things,
In humble places where others see nothing.

Keeping our eyes closed,
We can dream big without being dozed.
But the one barrier,
Is our heart, The Carrier.

In the era of Youth,
We may make mistakes in identifying the truth.
Should we not correct our faults?
Instead of shirking our duties and acting as truants.

Nature has immense power,
But it's us who need to ponder.
For they are present in our surroundings,
Enriching our lives and giving us a sense of
grounding.

8. Generational Grace

In wrinkled hands, wisdom's trace,
Generations meet and embrace.
Love's timeless dance, in every face,
Generational grace, a sacred space.

In tales, they weave, a legacy's lace,
Grandparents' whispers, time can't erase.
Their laughter echoes, in life's bustling pace,
Generational grace, in their embrace.

We find our peace being near them,
For their love and affection, they make us clem.
Laughing and giggling, the time we spend,
Unwinding the happiness we once hid under the
face dead.

These occasions are not mere,
These fleeting moments endow us with the
capacity for style and flair.
Enjoy the moments with your grandparents,
because you never know,
For what is there, left to happen tomorrow.

9. Gratitude's Symphony: Odes to Every Soul

I am grateful to you,
To all the parents, including mine,
Who raised their children, giving up all that they have.

I am grateful to you,
To all the siblings out there, whether it's the elder or younger one,
They bear our nuisance and crazy act,
Takes up our command and be irritated quite a few times.

I am grateful to you,
To all the house workers.
They are outsiders but yet are there to work for us.

I am grateful to you,
To all the teachers,
Who are in a journey of making their students a better version.

I am grateful to you,
To all the farmers working the entire day, in the field, Just to provide us with quality food.

I am grateful to the all the existing beings and their profession.
No job is small or big.
It depends on our perspective, of how we perceive.

10. Guiding Lights: A Tribute to Teachers

In classrooms bright, where minds take flight,
Amid the chalk dust, gleaming white,
Stands heroes tall, in wisdom's might,
Our teachers, beacons in our sight.

With patience vast, they sow the seeds,
In fertile minds, where dreams take the lead,
Through doubts and fears, they plant belief,
Igniting sparks, beyond relief.

Their lessons soar on wings of care,
Beyond the pages, they dare to share,
Life's truths, its tales, its highs, its lows,
In every word, a pearl of wisdom flows.

They are the shining souls, our mate,
They teach us different forms to create.
Always blessings us with words of joy,
In our tears of sadness, they never let us buoy.

11. Bound By Friendship

In laughter and tears, through highs and lows,
Best friends stick together, that's how it goes.

Sharing secrets, dreams, and silly schemes,
In our friendship, reality feels like dreams.

From late-night talks to inside jokes,
Our bond grows stronger with every poke.

Through thick and thin, we'll always stand,
Hand in hand, side by side, a lifelong band.

Beautiful is our friendship,
As long as we don't face a hardship.

Trusting each other is the key to strong relation,
And we will abide by it as our utmost passion.

12. A Language Of Love For Elder Brother

To my brother, near and far,
You are my shining star.
In every laugh and every tear,
Your love has been my guiding spear.

From scraped knees to broken hearts,
You've been there from the start.
With every step, through thick and thin,
Our bond is strong, it has always been.

You taught me how to climb and run,
To face the world and have some fun.
And when life's storms would rage and roar,
You stood by me, you were my shore.

Brothers, you're my heroes true,
In every shade of life's vast hue.
Your gentle strength and steady hand,
Have helped me grow, and have helped me stand.

So here's my thanks, my heart's song,
For all the times you've tagged along.
For all the love and laughs we share,
Dear brother, to you none can compare.

May life be kind, may dreams come true,
And know my love will follow you.
Through every joy, through every strife,
You're the best part of my life.

13. Little Brother, My Guiding Light

Little brother, with your eyes so bright,
In your laughter, I find my delight.
You look up to me, but can't you see?
It's you who inspires the best in me.

With every giggle, every playful chase,
You bring to our home such warmth and grace.
In your wide-eyed wonder and curious mind,
A world of magic, we together find.

You're the mischief in our mother's sigh,
The brave little soldier when you try.
With scraped knees and a will so strong,
You teach me what it means to belong.

In your dreams, I see myself reflected,
In your triumphs, I feel twice respected.
For every time you stumble and fall,
I'll be there for you, through it all.

So here's to you, my dear,
May your happy days be many, your sorrows few.
And know that no matter how far I roam,
You're my heart, my soul, my forever home.

Inward Spirals: Teenage Verse Unveiled

This is the second and the most chaotic phase of teenage life. It feels like the world has parted in two ways, negative and positive. We tend to lose our balance between happiness, excitement, and joy to navigating complex feelings of identity, self-worth, societal expectations, and self-doubt. It is a crucial time for all adolescents to look after themselves and stay healthy both physically and mentally. Let us revive all our true feelings and doubts.

Teenage years are like spirals turning inward; a journey of self-discovery, where every twist and turn is a lesson in love, life, and the intricate dance of growing up.

1. The Call To Rise

Behold, it has come to pass,
When your resolve was not at last.
The silent cries, a tale so true,
Fight for rights, that's what you must do.

Forge ahead, with honor's gleam,
Victory yours, in esteem's stream.

Now this state, each moment a question,
Unforeseen, this sense of regression.
Lost in doubts, every step a plight,
Why has your life dimmed, without its light?

On every floor, in every ideal's hall,
Living with grace, seems a distant call.

2. Lost Light: The Student's Soliluqe

In the shadowed halls where whispers fade,
Lies the tale of students' struggles, dismayed.
Beneath the weight of burdens, they sway,
As if shrouded by a dark, gloomy gray.

Each day a battle, unseen, unheard,
Their voices lost in the silence, absurd.
Discarded dreams, like fallen leaves,
Flutter aimlessly, no reprieve.

Their hearts, heavy with unspoken woes,
Echoing through empty corridors, they pose,
Questions unanswered, hopes deferred,
In the depths of despair, they're lured.

But in the midst of the darkest night,
A flicker of hope, a guiding light.
For even within the darkest cloud,
Resilient souls, determined, unbowed.

Through the storms of doubt and fear,
They rise, embracing what's unclear.
For within their struggles, they find,
Strength to endure, hearts intertwined.

So let their voices rise, bold and clear,
Breaking through the clouds, dispelling fear.
For in their struggles, they find their might,
Embracing the darkness, they shine bright.

3. Is It Okay To Not Be Okay?

I feel like drowning in the deepest emotions,
Draining all my feelings down.
I want to cry out loud,
But at the same time, I want to silence my cries.

Is it okay to not be okay?
Is it alright, if I silence the storms growing within me?
Is it well, if I draw back from carrying feelings for one? Is it fine to not be myself?

I tend to lose balance over my head,
Planning to keep everything down and jump onto my bed.
But that's just going to be a wish,
Because, yes, I don't dare to leave things unsolved.

Is It Okay To Not Be Okay?

I find myself clueless about what to do in life,
And at times I keep my mind ready with all I want to be. Isn't that weird to dream and arrange our future,
When I know that I will not achieve any?

Is It Okay To Not Be Okay?

I just feel yielding my thoughts and letting it flow,
Without keeping them captivated in my mind for decades.
But I am me, I can't get over my weakness,
If I try, I will, but am I valiant enough?

4. I Am Losing Myself Day By Day

I am losing myself,
In the jungles of thoughts,
Where no trees and plants reside,
But just my thoughts and me.

I want to be set free.
Free like those birds,
Chirping and singing, migrating to wherever they want, Without fearing to be lost.

But here stand I,
In front of the mirror all glossy,
I see a broken piece of ice,
And I am nowhere to be found in my reflection.

I wouldn't say that I am imperfect,
Because, in my imperfection,
Lies my little and smooth perfection.
And alas, I am bound by these words, roaming in my mind.

Feeling uplifted and joyful,
Just after I gave up on myself.
Strange, right?
But I found this thing to be a useful tool.

I am losing myself, yes,
But perhaps, in losing, I am found.

5. My Skin Felt Like A Sin

I hated my skin as it had pores and spots.
I hated my skin because it had dirt, of all the ones who embraced me.
I hated my skin being dark and tight.
And I kept hating myself because of my derm,
Until all went numb.

6. And They Say 'Boys Don't Cry'

Society tells boys, "Keep your feelings at bay,
Even if it breaks you, don't let them sway."

But why should they swallow their pain, day by
day? Aren't they allowed to feel, in their own way?

Yearning for freedom from this stifling decree,
Shouldn't they be granted the right to be free?

Their emotions, like whispers in a secret space,
Hidden behind a mask, they put on a brave face.

It's time for society to acknowledge the truth,
To break the cycle of suppression, uncouth.

Being stoic doesn't mean devoid of grace,
It's about owning our truths, in every embrace.

But after a long story being explained
They yet utter the same phrase, "Boys Don't Cry".

7. Lessons

Part by part,
In the dance of healing, we weave our broken hearts.

Way by way,
Truth hides behind veils of what people display.

Time by time,
Sweet promises turn sour, revealing the sublime.

Hour by hour,
From buds bloom, nature's gentle power.

Life flows like a river, and we must paddle along, embracing the twists and turns with courage and grace.

8. Cruel Summer

In the heat of a cruel summer's blaze,
Our hearts navigate a complex maze.

Emotions rise like waves upon the shore,
As we grapple with challenges, seeking more.

In this season of both joy and strife,
We learn to navigate the dance of life.

Through trials faced beneath the scorching sun,
We emerge stronger, and their journey begins.

9. Reflections Of Uncharted Self

Standing in front of the mirror,
Being clueless about what to work on.
Around people still feeling alone,
It feels like a place unknown.
Mirror, it will show my reflection right?
But what if it just puts before all my scars and questions? Will it still be called 'my' reflection?

I have nothing to do,
Every bit of my existence now feels like it's vanishing in the blue.
The blue of the sky,
Which I have to, someday say goodbye.
Wouldn't it be fun?
Being lost in the universe, between the moon and the sun.

10. The Ascent Of Ambition

In the heart of youth where dreams ignite,
A teenager stands, a beacon bright.
With eyes cast forward, a fervent gaze,
They seek the summit through the haze.

Ambitions high as the endless sky,
On wings of hope, they aim to fly.
Each step a leap towards goals vast,
Thriving for the best, not chained to the past.

The climb is steep, the path unsure,
Yet their resolve remains ever pure.
For every fall, a lesson learned,
With every triumph, respect earned.

In the mirror of time, they see their rise,
Not a soul deterred by the size.
Of challenges faced or fears to quell,
In their heart, a victorious yell.

So let the world watch and see,
This teenager's spirit, wild and free.
Thriving for the best, with all their might,
Turning every darkness into light.

11. It Is Pouring On The Inside

It's raining, it's pouring,
My soul seems to be snoring.
Leaving me with all sorts or scars,
It feels to be resting in some bars.

It's raining, it's pouring.
Waiting for my happiness to wake up is boring.
Trembling and unsolved chords,
These are perfect examples of wounding words.

It's raining, it's pouring,
My sadness greets me, with a welcome as warm
as if it was outpouring.
Beneath my smile, a storm is forming,
Tears like raindrops, quietly storming.

12. Lost In Appearance

In striving to keep up with other's facade,
I pulled on their guise, a mockery I would applaud.
Pretending to be what I'm not, just to shine,
Yet in the spotlight, I even lost what was mine.

Thoughts about the future danced in my head,
But riches of self-lay buried, unread.
In the middle of the noise, I was lost in the crowd,
I wandered, between voices too loud.

I feel caught in the trap of other's designs,
I wandered, searching everything, but not the one that was mine.
A strange self-drifted and unsure,
In the mirror, I see a reflection obscure.

Lost in the echo of other's applause,
I desire to break free from these laws.
Seeking solace, in the middle of the clamor's drone,
Now I found my voice, reclaiming my own.

In the stillness, I began to see,
The beauty of being me.
No longer chained to appearance's guise,
I stepped into the truth, where my own spirit flies.

13. Stance Of A Rustic Girl

The way I am always discarded,
I am asked to be silent.
And then they say,
"You have everything you ever wanted".

I want to ask those people,
Are you talking about the discrimination I face, just for being a girl?
Are you talking about me being abandoned?
If yes, I have never wished to have this treatment.

Am I born to be the shoe under a man's feet?
Can I not be free to show up what I can be?
It's alright, to be honest!
Because I know that I am being raised to change the scenario,

I may be a little teenager,
But my dreams?
No, I rather name it, reality,
So I am here to enlighten my path in this real world.

In the real world where each item is fake,
I am going to bake, my own piece of cake.

14. Finding Beauty in Life's Rollercoaster

You know, life is like this crazy rollercoaster ride that you never asked to be on, but once you're in, you realize it's the most amazing adventure ever.

Even when it feels like everything's falling apart, there's this beauty in the chaos, you know? Like those moments when the sun sets painting the sky in shades of pink and orange, or when you're with your friends, laughing until your stomach hurts, and for a split second, nothing else matters. It's those little moments that make all the struggles worth it.

Life throws curveballs at us all the time, but it's on us to swing for the fences. And even if we strike out sometimes, we gotta keep stepping up to the plate because, in the end, it's the game that counts, not just the score.

15. To The World

In the hush of midnight's embrace, I whisper my heart's refrain,
A symphony of dreams that dance amidst the gentle rain.
In shadows, casted by moonlight's glow, I bare my soul's true plight,
A longing song that yearns to soar beyond the depths of night.

Oh, world, hear my tender plea, from this adolescent heart,
Where innocence and passion meet, where dreams and fears depart.
For in the silence of my youth, I find my voice anew,
A melody of hope and truth, a beacon shining through.

Through the maze of tangled thoughts, I navigate with grace,
Embracing every twist and turn, every challenge I embrace.
For though the road wind may bend, uncertainty may reign,

I'll journey forth with courage bold, unshackled from the chain.

So let my words like petals fall upon the winds of time, A testament to love's embrace, a testament to prime.
For in this fleeting moment, as adolescence fades away, I'll cherish every heartbeat, every tear, and every day.

So here I stand, a teenager so bold, with dreams as vast as the sea,
A humble soul, a warrior's heart, in search of destiny.
And though the path ahead may be uncertain, dark, and steep,
I'll face it all with open arms, for in my heart, I keep.

So world, I offer you this piece of talk, this humble plea, A testament to love's sweet song, to hope's eternal key.
For in the end, when shadows fade, and dawn's first light shall gleam,
I'll rise above, I'll soar beyond, in pursuit of my dream.

Whispers of Young Hearts

Love's like that fluttery feeling in your stomach when you see your crush in the hallway. It's like your heart does a happy dance when they smile at you. You know it's real when you can't stop thinking about them when their name makes you blush like crazy. Teenage affection is like sharing secrets under the stars, stealing glances in class, and writing each other notes that you keep hidden like treasures. It's giggles and whispers with your besties about that cute guy or girl. It's holding hands and feeling like you're floating on air. Love as a teen is all-consuming, messy, and beautiful, filled with highs and lows that you ride like a rollercoaster. I know It's scary but it is exciting and absolutely worth it.

And then there's this part, where the love turns into pain. It's like, we were two pieces of a puzzle, but suddenly, the picture changed. He was my world, my everything. Texting till midnight, giggling secrets under the stars. Then, whispers turned into arguments, love faded into silence. Tears blurred our once bright future. It's hard to explain how it feels when someone you thought would be your forever suddenly becomes a memory. But I'm learning to let go, to find myself amidst the pieces of us left behind. It's like growing pains of the heart, but I'm still learning to breathe without him.

In love's embrace, laughter and silent looks speak a shared language of the heart, where every hug feels like home.

Love is the thread that stitches our lives together, a silent strength that softens life's sharp corners, weaving us into a shared story of moments and memories.

Breakups are like the bitter medicine of life, they taste harsh, but within them lies the cure for a stronger heart, the wisdom to cherish what's next, and the courage to love again.

1. Starry Nights of Teenage Love

Underneath the night's soft glow,
In whispered words, our love would grow.
Hand in hand, we'd stroll the street,
Sharing dreams, our hearts would meet.

Laughter ringing in the air,
Moments shared without a care.
With each smile, our bond would thrive,
In this world, just you and I.

Teenage love, pure and bright,
Guiding us through darkest night.
With every beat, our love would soar,
Forever together, now and evermore.

2. Fate's Embrace

Once in our history,
He asked me if I could be there for him throughout,
And I answered nodding my head as if I was
saying 'yes' But I should let him know that I,
myself have lost me.
How could I promise him to be by his side forever,
'Lee'?

He uttered a few words,
Making me feel that maybe he wants me back.
But soon I realized, that returning was never an
option for me
It was late, indeed I was late,
However, that was the fate.

A silent fighter he was,
Who then turned into a violent one.
Figuring out the reason is difficult,
But gathering the courage to believe it was him,
Better to say his new version was even more
devastating.

But me? I would still be with him no matter what,
Because the love I have for my love holds more power than any hate.

3. Love's First Glimpse

The moment I saw her, it was like magic,
Heart racing, emotions erratic.
Her smile, it lit up the darkest night,
And suddenly, everything felt right.

In her eyes, I found a universe so vast,
A love so pure, it was destined to last.
With every beat of my heart, I knew,
It was like a dream come true.

Love at first sight, they call it fate,
But with her, it's more than just a date.
This love for you is never going to fade,
Even when we are under the fall of a cascade.

In a fleeting glance, our souls danced, igniting
fates in a single stance.
Eyes met, hearts set, in love's net, forever
entwined without regret.
It's a feeling, deep and true,
My dear, forever and always, I'll be loving you.

4. Silent Symphony

In the dance of hearts, a silent rift did grow,
Two souls entwined, yet destined not to know,
He, with love tender, sought to hold her near,
She, in her longing, craved a different sphere.

In the garden of affection, they both tread,
But the petals of understanding remained unread,
He whispered in gestures, soft and kind,
Yet failed to fathom the echoes of her mind.

Yet amidst the ache, a bittersweet truth,
In their flaws, they found a shared root,
For love's true essence, they both now see,
Resides in embracing each other's mystery.

Though their paths may diverge, love remains,
A gentle reminder amidst life's strains,
For in the dance of hearts, where
misunderstandings reside,
Lies the beauty of love, ever ready to abide.

5. Whispers in the Café

In the dim of night, where shadows dance and play,
Two souls converge in a cafe's quiet sway.
Unbeknownst to them, fate's tender thread weaves,
As hearts awaken to the love it conceives.

But a barrier rose, unseen yet strong,
Tearing them apart, where they once belonged.
Reasons unknown, they dare not investigate,
As destiny weaves its spell, sealing their fate.

In the same dim cafe, where they once found bliss,
They meet again, hearts heavy with aching miss.
Deciding to part, though love still lingers deep,
They hide their pain, the secret they both keep.

Despite their resolve, emotions intertwine,
A love forbidden yet refuses to resign.
In the depths of their souls, a silent plea,
To hold on tight, to set their love free.

6. Eternal Melody

Love, it is a word so simple but profound,
A feeling that makes our hearts abound.
It's an affection that moves us to greater heights,
And fills our days and nights with light.

Love is like the sun that warms our soul,
The moon that guides us towards our goal.
It is the breeze that soothes our troubled mind,
And the rain that washes away all our binds.

Love is the melody of life's sweetest song,
A symphony that carries all of us along.
It's the rhyme that beats in every heart,
And the spark that ignites every start.

Love is the beauty that we see around,
In every sight, in every sound.
It's the pure magic that makes our life worthwhile,
And the spark of hope that makes us smile.

Let us all cherish this gift of love,
And hold it close like a precious and warm glove.
Let it guide us, on life's journey ahead,
And lead us towards a brighter path instead.

7. A Girl In Brunette

The way she looks at me,
My heart trembles like it isn't free.
Capturing my pics in her pretty eyes,
Is what she says, to her, it satisfies.
But more beautiful are those eyes,
That holds a vision over me and never denies.
For longer than hours,
Even at the bars,
Making me feel loved always,
By her strong and affectionate gaze.

This beautiful brunette has my heart,
And more adorable than her is no one in the chart.
The way her hair goes to and fro,
Makes me mesmerized and frozen no less than snow.
No one else knows what she feels for me, but I.
Never her eyes or words to me are going to lie.

Her shadow chases me unfailingly,
And every day I fall for her more and more unknowingly.
This Asian Brunette,
Hiding in her duvet,

Stole the whole of me.

She wants to be called as my baby bear,
But little does she knows that a tigress is growing within her.
Yes my love, I'm lost in your eyes,
The love I carry for you is something no one denies.

I never realized how frozen I was for days,
Until you melted me with your warm embrace.
I will love you more and more,
Until the horizon meets the sea shore.

8. Whispers Of A Fading Flame

Our romantic memory is obviously a haunting ghost,
A love that was passionate, but could not host.
It was a love that so deep, but could not sustain,
It was a love that was beautiful, but ended in pain.

It's a memory that tastes, both sweet and bitter,
A love that was boundlessly perfect, but could not glitter.
It was a passion that burned, but could not survive,
It was a love that was so incredible, but could not thrive.

It reminds me of a love that was worth the suffocation and pain,
It was a love that was pure, but ended without any gain.
It was a love that was deep, but could not take flight,
It was a love that was amazing, but could not see the light.

It teaches us that all love stories are not always easy, That it can be messy, and sometimes it's abruptly breezy. That even in the darkest of days, a spark can ignite,
And give us a flicker of hope, and make us see the light.

Won't you cherish our romantic memory,
And let it guide us through life's unknown mystery.
For it reminds us that love is worth all the pain,
And that even in dim, love can still and always remain.

I found a love, for me
Darling, just dive right in and follow my lead
Well, I found a girl, beautiful and sweet
Oh, I never knew you were the someone waiting for me
'Cause we were just kids when we fell in love
Not knowing what it was
I will not give you up this time
But darling, just kiss me slow
Your heart is all I own
And in your eyes, you're holding mine

Extracted from a song by Ed Sheeran, named 'Perfect'

9. Love By Chance

In this universe so vast,
Our paths crossed by chance,
And in that single moment,
Our love began to dance.

The stars aligned for us,
Our destiny intertwined,
And we found each other,
In a world so unrefined.

Our love grew stronger,
With every passing day,
And we knew in our hearts,
That it was meant to stay.

So here we are together,
Two souls now as one,
Blessed by chance,
And by love's sweetest bond.

10. Love's Serendipity

Love's serendipity, a fateful chance,
An unexpected twist of circumstance,
Two hearts that beat as one, in perfect sync,
A love that knows no bounds, nor end, nor brink.

With every moment spent, we grow closer still,
Our love a flame that burns with endless thrill,
And though the world may change, and time may
pass, Our love will stay forever, an unbreakable
bond to last.

So let us cherish every moment, every breath,
And love each other until the very end of our
quest,
For in this universe so vast, so vast and grand,
Our love by chance, will always take a stand.

11. Can We Fall In Love Like They Do In Movies

Can we fall in love like they do in movies? It's a question that lingers in the hearts of many, as they watch the on-screen characters meet, fall in love, and live happily ever after. The idea of love at first sight, of a connection that can't be denied, is a romantic notion that captures our imagination and fills our hearts with hope.

We watch these movies, and we dream of finding our own fairytale love story. We imagine meeting someone who will sweep us off our feet, who will understand us in a way that no one else can, and who will love us unconditionally. We dream of romantic moments, of candlelit dinners, of long walks on the beach, and of stolen kisses in the rain.

But can we really fall in love like they do in movies? Is it possible to find that kind of connection, that kind of love, in real life?

The truth is, falling in love is a complicated process. It's not something that happens overnight, and it's not always easy. It requires getting to know someone on a deeper level, building a connection over time, and working through the challenges that arise along the way.

But that doesn't mean that real-life love can't be just as beautiful as the love stories we see on-screen. In fact, it can be even more beautiful, because it's real. It's messy, it's imperfect, and it's full of surprises, but it's also full of joy, of laughter, and of genuine human connection.

12. Shades Of Belief

'My happiness depends on you',
I said when it was true.
Now I no longer believe in this phrase,
As you have pulled yourself out of the fight,
We were having that night

Do you remember the last time,
When you took my name out of your glossy lips?
I turned red!
It felt like the one who was starting to accept the reality was dead.

I was driven deep into delusion,
And found no solution.

13. A Plea for Change

I never wanted you to leave me like a used bag,
Giving me a ride and putting loads of tag.
It just feels like years when you isolate yourself from the world,
I still couldn't figure it out
Whether it was your healing period or a battle you fought.
I am running out of words about how I feel about your changed behaviors.
'Don't go to him' was the only line buzzing in my mind in chorus,
Tell me, if I should wait for you to return?
Can I still have a part of you that you said was once mine?
Can you stop drinking people's blood like you drink wine?
Can you stop being violent?

14. Love's Illusion

Dream it was for me
When he said that he loved me,
And I know, that was a thought of vain with no meaning behind it.
He thinks I'll be happy being with someone else,
But little does he know what love is,
Maybe cause he never did.
I'm still stuck with feelings and memories that remind me of him,
Every day and night.
He is the only one I want to have a vision of,
Before sleeping and after waking up in the morning. With this feeling, I have to fight,
Whether it is or not in my might.
For him, love is nothing but a doll,
With which he can play whenever he wants,
Whoever he can give without hesitation.
For love to him is just sensual pleasure and all other things are leisure.

15. Confessions of a Reformed Heart

She thinks I am here just to have fun with the person I love,
But is this the real meaning of love?
No, right?
And I understand that.
I won't deny that I was a playboy,
But I was never the same with her.
I gave my best to prove it to her,
That my love for her is unconditional.
She just takes what and how I am reacting,
Can she not look over my past self, and focus on what I am today?
I am not a born God,
I am not perfect,
And honestly, no human being is perfect.
Why don't people understand?
Is it not self-explanatory?
I want to let her know, that I am not the one to be violent without reason.
I am going through a lot.
And these feelings are unavoidable.
Can I please have a chance to skip this phase of life?

I want to be normal.
I want to be back to what I was.
I don't want to lose the only love of my life.

16. Veiled Reminiscence

He found peace in being alone,
But I missed his face, the joy I've known.
His charm was warm, a cozy fire,
Held my heart, lifted me higher.

Now I look at him, lost in thought,
The love we had, now seems for naught.
Where did it go, that soft, sweet glow?
Left me in pieces, feeling low.

The face that smiled at our start,
Now breaks my heart, tears it apart.
But his touch, soft as a breeze,
Stays in my mind, puts me at ease.

Our laughter and tears, woven tight,
His spirit's with me, day and night.
Though we're apart, we're still combined,
In a love that's forever signed.

17. Unspoken Symphony

In every breath, a silent song,
A melody of love that's lifelong.
With words unspoken, hearts entwine,
In love's embrace, our souls align.

Through whispered sighs and tender gaze,
In love's embrace, our spirits raise.
No need for words to paint the sky,
Our love, a bond that'll never die.

18. Forever Dance

Just you and me, under the moon's soft light,
Dancing close, holding each other tight.
The world fades away, it's just us tonight,
In this dance, everything feels so right.

Your laugh, a sound that's pure and true,
It's the simple things that I love about you.
We move together, our love in plain sight,
In this dance, our hearts take flight.

No grand gestures, just this quiet space,
Our little corner, our own special place.
With every step, our love's story we write,
In this forever dance, our love shines bright.

So let's keep dancing, through life's twists and turns, With you by my side, my heart no longer yearns.
In this dance, we're perfectly aligned,
Our simple, forever love, defined.

19. Eternal Embrace

Love's embrace, powerful yet weak,
Sometimes bold and sometimes meak.
Patients in abundance,
A pretty and impressive glance.

Warmth of my heart,
She is a work of art.
Beautiful and impressive,
Her gestures acting as a force too adhesive.

My mind has no peace,
But her soft embrace puts me as ease.

20. Whispers of the Heart

In love's warm clasp, our hearts find peace,
Secrets softly shared, crafting a vessel so sacred.
Over dales and peaks, our journey's lease,
In love's soft nest, our souls are cradled and
treasured.

With each murmur, a vow we entrust,
In love's embrace, our worries dissolve.
No shadow too vast, no dusk too robust,
Love guides us home, in its mystery we revolve.

21. Infinite Love

Blocks of cement when tucked together,
Called it is a house so sweet.
But allowing my heart to be free,
I cannot believe me.

Bonds so sweet and beautiful we build,
To race our hearts we make a strong field.
Embracing each other till the last minute of the midnight, Peaceful sleep crossing sight.

In building bonds, we find our home,
Where hearts are free to roam.
Through laughter shared and tears we've shed,
In love's embrace, our souls are fed.

With every moment, our relation grows,
In each phase, our passion shows.
No obstacle too great, no hurdle too high,
With love as our compass, we'll never say goodbye.

You promised the world and I fell for it
I put you first and you adored it
Set fires to my forest
And you let it burn
Sang off-key in my chorus
'Cause it wasn't yours

Extracted from a song by Selena Gomez, named 'Lose You To Love Me'

22. Farewell Symphony

In the silence of goodbye, echoes linger,
A symphony of heartache, fingers on the trigger.
Our love, once a melody sweet and pure,
Now fades into the night, a distant lure.

With every word unspoken, a tear is shed,
In the silence of goodbye, our love is dead.
No encore, no final bow,
Just the echo of goodbye, haunting us now.

23. Broken Vows

In the ashes of our love, lies a broken vow,
Promises shattered, dreams disavow.
What once burned bright, now flickers low,
In the chill of goodbye, we let each other go.

With every whispered goodbye, a piece of me dies,
In the ashes of our love, love's flame denies.
No redemption, no second chance,
Just the remnants of love's bittersweet dance.

24. Empty Echoes

In our goodbye, echoes sound,
Singing of sadness, tears all around.
Our love, once a safe place, now just empty space,
In the quiet of farewell, we release our embrace.

Each echo brings back the past,
In our goodbye, love doesn't last.
No comfort, no safe place to be,
Just the echoes of a love that's now free.

25. Torn Pages

In the chapters of our love, we are left with pages torn,
A story that is unfinished, hearts forlorn.
What once held promises, now holds only pain,
In this final chapter, I write our refrain.

With every tear-stained page, a part I have to separate and it is said,
That in the chapters of our love, dreams shred.
No post scripts, no happy end,
Left with broken pieces we can't mend.

The end was classified by pain and regression,
Our story ended here and nothing could be done.

26. Fading Stars

In the sky of our love, stars go dim,
A group of stars lost, like a forgotten hymn.
What used to glow, now slowly fades,
In the night of goodbyes, our love downgrades.

Each star that dims takes a memory too,
In our love's sky, dreams fall through.
No more wishes on stars, no bright streak,
Just the dimming stars, as our love grows weak.

27. Pouring With You

When I see that it is raining,
Once again I want to feel the moment of us
pouring. Pouring in with you,
Side by side walking on drops of dew.
Feeling lively and fresh,
Under the rain that was for today set.
As the rain stopped showering the droplets of
water, Your image started to dull and become
shorter.
It was the time I realized,
Rain needs to stop and so do we.
We need to stop pouring in with each other,
Or I would rather say, I need to stop puring in with
your image.

28. Journey through Heartache and Hope

In a realm where dusk's soft veil descends,
My spirit seeks the hues that daylight lends.
Each dawn unfolds as a silent fray,
Where dreams are pressed beneath burdens gray.
Fragile hopes, like glass, I clutch in fear,
As I wander a labyrinth, no compass near.
Through shadowed halls of doubt I roam,
Alone amidst the throng, unseen, unknown.

Yet, in the tempest's eye, beauty's spark ignites,
In shared laughter, secrets, and empathetic sights.
These fleeting gems, they whisper clear,
"You tread not alone," and draw me near
To a beacon's promise, slicing through the night,
Guiding me beyond the shadows, towards the light.
In these precious instants, when gazes lock and blend,
I find peace in love's potential, a kindred spirit, a friend.

Life's grand mosaic, interwoven with strands of gold, Love, the harmonious anthem, brave and

bold.
Through sorrow's tears and the ache of parting's throe,
I cling to the hope that love's seed may yet grow.
For in the vastness of time and space, I trust,
There's a soul that mirrors mine, pure and just.
With every step upon this path, my heart's door swings wide,
Embracing the dance of love, through the ebb and tide.

For in love's enduring flame, I find my strength renewed,
A constant, shining force, through trials pursued.
So I journey forth, with hope as my guide,
Believing in love's power, vast and wide.
For love, in its essence, is life's sweet refrain,
A symphony of joy, transcending pain.

29. Heartbeat Of Youth

In the whirlwind of youth, where dreams soar high,
I stand, a teen, with a message for the sky.
With a heart unscarred and hope in my eyes,
I speak of love, pure, without disguise.

“Believe in love,” I shout to the stars above,
For it’s the one thing that we all can dream of.
It’s not just a tale for the old or the meek,
But a truth we seek, that gives strength to the weak.

Love’s not a game, it’s not fleeting or slight,
It’s a beacon that guides us through the darkest night.
It’s the laughter that echoes in the silent halls,
The hand that lifts you, whenever you fall.

To the world, I say, with all my youthful might,
Love is the dawn that follows the longest night.
It’s the courage that whispers when you’re about to give in,
The melody that plays when life’s symphony begins.

Come, let's hold on to love, let's cherish its light,
Let's carry it forward, through the day and night.
For love is the essence, the core of our being,
A force ever-present, all-knowing, all-seeing.

As a teen, I believe, and I want you to see,
That love is the answer, for you and for me.
It's the journey, the destination, the story that's told,
The fire that warms us, when the world feels cold.

So here's my plea, from the heart of the young,
Let love be the language, on every tongue.
For in this belief, our spirits will thrive,
With love as our compass, we'll truly be alive.

30. The Distance You Asked For

In the quiet space between us, where once laughter used to dance,
Lies a chasm wide and silent, filled with longing, filled with chance.
You've asked for room to breathe, to find the solace of your own,
Yet in this newfound distance, I've never felt more alone.

Your words, they echo softly, like a whisper in the night,
"Let's tread a path less crowded, let our hearts take gentle flight."
But my heart clings to the shadows, to the warmth we used to share,
In the stillness of your absence, I find solace nowhere.

I respect your need for space, for a moment to unwind, Yet every step you take away, is a tether that unwinds. The closeness that we cherished, now a memory so dear, Becomes a silent symphony that only I can hear.

I'll honor your request, your need to find your peace,
But know that in this quiet, my love will never cease. For even as you wander, in your solitude apart,
You carry with you always, a piece of my heart.

So go ahead and journey, find the answers that you seek, I'll be here in the silence, strong in love, though I feel weak.
And should you glance behind you, in the echoes of our past,
You'll find me in the distance, loving you to the last.

31. Elixir Of Soul

In life's grand feast, where flavors blend,
There lies a spice we can't pretend.
A magical ingredient, so pure and true,
It's love, the essence of every hue.

It's not in riches, nor in gold,
But in the warmth, when hands we hold.
In every smile, in tears that dry,
Love's the magic that money can't buy.

It stirs the soul, it lights the dark,
A silent whisper in the heart's own park.
It's the laughter shared in the pouring rain,
The balm that soothes the deepest pain.

In every chapter, every line of our story,
Love's the ink that writes our glory.
It's the compass when we lose our way,
The dawn that heralds a brand new day.

Let's sprinkle love, let's make it spread,
From the mountain's peak to the ocean's bed.
In this journey, from start to end,
Love's the magic, our eternal friend.

In the tapestry of moments, woven so fine,
Love's the thread that makes life shine.
A spell so potent, it can't be seen,
Yet in its absence, where would we have been?

Here's to love, in all its might,
The truest magic, in plain sight.
For in the end, when all is done,
It's love that's victorious, love that's won.

32. Unified Hearts

In lands of vibrant nights and sunlit skies,
Where laughter dances in my people's eyes,
There is a bond, it is a love that's true,
In every heart, it's leaves an essence that we can't undo.

My people, they are dear to me,
In their embrace, I find myself free.
From ancient stories to modern song,
Their spirit echoes strong and long.

In fields all beautiful with flowers bright,
They stand tall with grace from morning to night,
Their hands weave dreams, their souls entwine,
In every breath, a legacy divine.

Through trials fierce and storms untamed,
My people rise, their courage proclaimed.
With unity as their guiding light,
They conquer shadows, banish night.

In celebrations grand and humble abodes,
My people gather, hearts bestowed,
With love that binds, with hope that soars,
In every step, a promise roars.

Oh, how I cherish my people's embrace,
Their essence, their rhythm, their steadfast grace.
For in their love, I find my home,
In every heartbeat, I am known.

So let us sing, let us rejoice,
In my people's love, let us find our voice.
For in this bond, forever strong,
We journey together, where we belong.

Enlightened Pathways

In the depths of our journey, "Enlightened Pathways" isn't just a title; it's our story revealed through poetries—the struggles, triumphs, and the lessons learned. It encapsulates the raw emotions of adolescence: the fear of not fitting in, the weight of expectations, and the flicker of hope that persists.

This story is for every teenager who's felt lost, reminding them they're not alone. In its pages, we find solace, inspiration, and the courage to keep moving forward. It's a journey of self-discovery, where each step brings us closer to embracing our true selves. Through the highs and lows, we're reminded of our resilience, our capacity to grow, and the beauty of finding light in the darkest of times. So let's walk this path together, knowing that within its twists and turns, we'll find the strength to shine brightly, illuminating our own enlightened pathways.

Being unique takes courage, but it's as simple as being true to yourself in a world full of copies.

1. The Uncharted Course

In the realm of youth where dreams take flight,
A path unfolds in the shivering night.
With steps unsure, we commence our quest,
Each heart embarks on its own zest.

Through the thicket of doubts and fears,
We navigate the sea of adolescent years.
The compass of our soul points to the dawn,
Guiding us where our true selves are drawn.

In the silence of the stars, we find our voice,
Whispering tales of struggle, and rejoice.
For every tear that waters the ground,
A seed of strength is profoundly found.

Let us come together to sow the seed,
Of our courage and all good deed.
Don't leave desire, don't lose courage,
To each other, let's encourage.

2. The Echo Of Silence

Being a teen is quiet in a noisy way,
We hear our thoughts, even what they don't say.
In the quiet, our true selves we find,
Showing the grace that's been there all the time.

Life's loud with what others expect us to be,
But our own quiet song rises up, wild and free.
It's when things are calm, we can really see,
What we hope for and dream, what we want to be.

Our quiet wishes, they have a special power,
To lift us up, make us strong, help us flower.
With every quiet step, we find our own beat,
And learn to dance, rain or shine, feeling sweet.

3. The Weight Of Dreams

Heavy is the crown of dreams we wear,
A regal burden we're chosen to bear.
With aspirations high and spirits brave,
We march towards the future we crave.

The weight of dreams, a constant test,
To prove our mettle and be our best.
Yet, in this load, we're not confined,
For in our dreams, our wings are designed.

So let us carry our dreams with pride,
For they are the stars by which we guide.
In their heft, we find our flight,
Soaring into our destiny's light.

4. The Flicker Of Hope

In the darkest of nights, a flicker glows,
A little beacon where hope freely flows.
It's the spark that ignites the fire within,
A testament to where we've been and where we'll begin.

This flicker, a guide through the shadow's dance,
Leads us to give our dreams a fighting chance.
For even the smallest flame can defy the dark,
Illuminating the journey of every heart.

Let this flicker of hope be our eternal flame,
A light that no hardship can ever tame.
With each step, let it grow and spread,
Until the path ahead is brightly lit and widely tread.

5. The Tapestries Of Trials

Life's a mix of happy and hard days,
Like a quilt with many shades.
Each piece is a story of our life,
Sewn with care, through joy and strife.

We're strong and kind, all the way,
Our tales tell of our bright and gray.
Each challenge we face and pass,
Strengthens our bond, like strong glass.

In our quilt, tough times glitter,
Showing dreams aren't always bitter.
With every bump on our street,
Our life's story becomes more neat.

6. The Dance Of Resilience

Resilience, a rhythm that pulses deep,
A dance of the heart, a leap and sweep.
With every fall, we rise anew,
Graceful in recovery, our strength we renew.

The dance of resilience, a beautiful art,
A choreography of courage, a vital part.
In the ballet of life, we twirl and sway,
Embracing each movement, come what may.

So let us dance with resilience bold,
In the story of our lives, yet to be told.
For in this dance, we find our way,
To rise and shine, day after day.

7. The Whisper Of Growth

Growth whispers softly in the winds of change,
A gentle murmur, both strange and derange.
It's the essence that allows us to change ourselves,
A view point where every teenager indulge themselves.

With every whisper, we stretch our mind and reach,
We learn lessons that only time can teach.
Growth is indeed like the musical song,
That guides us to the place we belong.

Let us heed the whisper, subtle and clear,
For in its message, our path appears.
With every whisper, we grow and thrive,
In the garden of life, where we're alive.

8. The Embrace Of Self

When we hug ourselves, we find a quiet place,
A spot where worries just erase.
Right there, feeling good in our skin,
We find the strength that's always been within.

Loving ourselves, strong and true,
Tells a tale of being okay with you.
In this hug, we're really free,
To be the person we choose to be.

Let's treat ourselves kind, and full of care,
In our own hug, we find what's fair.
With happiness and calm, life's gentle pace,
In the cozy hug of our own embrace.

9. The Light In Darkness

Even when it's really dark, there's always a little light,
A soft glow that the night can't hide.
It's the light inside us, warm and true,
A little spark that helps us make it through.

This light shows how strong we really are,
Shining bright like a little star.
It's when things seem the darkest that our light can shine,
Leading the way, time after time.

We should keep this light shining every day,
Because it's a part of us in every way.
With this light, we find our way through,
Lighting up paths that feel brand new.

10. The Journey Together

Together we walk on this path of life,
Companions through joy and strife.
Hand in hand, heart to heart,
In our unity, we find our art.

The journey together, a shared quest,
In the company of others, we're at our best.
For in the mirror of each other's soul,
We see the reflections that make us whole.

Let's conclude the voyage, side by side,
In the fellowship of life, let us abide.
For on this path, we're never alone,
Together, we find our way home.

11. The Key To Success

Keep your mind calm,
Place relief upon your palm.
Where burdens are your loads,
Set sail on new roads.

Life's like the ocean, big and wide,
A place where dreams can't hide.
Just like fish swim down below,
You can reach high, and let your spirit glow.

Success is like a bird, flying free,
Up in the sky, where it loves to be.
Out of the cage, into the air,
It shows us that winning's not so rare.

In every heart, a dream can wake,
Even when the journey's tough to take.
Step by step, the way gets bright,
To the things we love, that feel just right.

So, let's open our arms, and touch the sky,
On changing winds, we'll learn to fly.
Success is close, it's ours to keep,
So let's jump in, take the leap.

~Our Struggles~

1. Marks and Us

The corners of midnight which are silent, where the world is sound asleep, and dreams are just barely stepping out, contain a student, a silent warrior.
Their battle is not with swords or shields; it is in the sacred classrooms where the air is filled with the smell of chalk dust and expectations that are left unstated.
They can only be seen with the weight of textbooks on their back like Atlas, their spine bent under the heavy load of quadratic equations and historical dates.
Their fingers torture the leaves, gathering comfort in the inked words or indeed they are the only friends who do not judge us or ask for more than we can give them.

From all directions "they" hurry to the gatherings that are staged in the presence of the nearest and dearest to their families, they scour the report cards urgently like the hawks are hunting their prey.
"Your GPA is?" they inquire as if it were a crystal ball epiphany.
The student smiles, teeth clenched, and makes up a story like, "Everything is fine." But underneath the

exterior lies the truth, in fact, a hurricane begins to brew, a cycle of self-distrust and an inferiority complex.

"They" act like unforgiving judges, use red pens to mark slash and circle essays. They sometimes annotate "Can do better," not knowing that each of those red marks is a bullet through the student's heart.

They cannot see the weary nights, the flashing screen, the coffee-stained notes, the fervent quest for knowledge.

For "them", success consists of numbers, percentages, rankings, test scores. They are only trying to help.

They mean well, of course, they want the child to soar higher than they ever did.

But who knows of shaking hands during exams, who listens to the half-hushed prayers, who deals with the universe for at least one extra point? Beyond all this, lies our emotion that stays thrashed.

The student, on the other hand, when the target is missed, and the arrow falls down, remnants all alone.

They paint on a face that is fearless, fortitude masks that are the norms for growing up. It is not sensitivity to be shown, the only admissible thing is strength that is akin to an encryption code for the adults' world.

And indeed, these are the wounds! They go deeper and are engraved in the heart. Taunts fall down on kids like acid rain, eating away at their confidence. "Why can't you be like her? She does so well!" is a common line they repeat as if comparison was a sport.

The student takes the hit, their heart is a punching bag. They give a nod, a smile, and step away only to their room, where books are flooded with their silent tears.

Can the scar fade away? Perhaps, it will, with time, but the fear? The gnawing fear of falling short, it doesn't go away. It quietly speaks when all else has their peace, in the night, when the world is dark and the planet is asleep.

"What If you are not enough?" it inquires. The student, who is mashed in the folds of blankets and uncertainty, struggles into tears.

That's why I toast to them, the unsung heroes, the ones who fight against invisible enemies, who carefully keep dreams like a piece of glass. They should be able to find strength in their difficulty and resilience in their tears. Because in their hearts a story is kept, a story of surviving, of courage, of humans who are more than numbers.

Let's strive to be the best. We will live our life instead of surviving. We will take good care of people who speak the words of fire today. Let's Promise To Be Proud Of Ownself!

2. I am not a Captive, Please let me be Free

In my mind, thoughts twist and turn,
Like leaves in a breeze, they churn.
Things I can't share, they weigh me down,
In a world where smiles can hide a frown.

At home, it's like I'm trapped in a cage,
No escape from this never-ending stage.
They say, "Stay inside, don't waste your time,
There's so much to do, don't cross the line."

But outside's where I find some peace,
Where worries fade and my thoughts release.
A chance to walk, to breathe the air,
To feel like life's more than just a stare.

"Why go out?" they always say,
"You could do this, that, any day."
But being cooped up, it suffocates,
I need space to roam, to appreciate.

I long for moments under the open sky,
Where I can be me, not just pass by.
To hear the birds, to feel the sun,
To know there's more to life than just getting things done.

Parents and friends, I'm not asking for much,
Just a chance to escape from this constant clutch.
To wander, to ponder, to make memories,
To learn about life beyond what everyone sees.

In this struggle of wants and what's right,
I seek understanding, not just a fight.
To find my place, to grow and learn,
To find myself, to feel the burn.

So please, hear my plea, don't shut me in,
Let me stretch my wings, let me begin.
To explore the world, to find my way,
To refresh my soul, day by day.

For I am human, with dreams to chase,
In this journey of life, I'll find my space.
To laugh, to cry, to simply be,
To embrace each moment, to feel free.

3. Colors Of Emotions

I feel like I'm drowning in the deepest blues,
Sinking beneath waves of uncertainty and
confusion.
My emotions swirl like the stormy sea,
Dragging me down into depths I can't see.

Is it okay to not be okay?
In the midnight blue of my mind's ocean,
I'm lost in a labyrinth of doubt and emotion.
But even in the darkest depths,
I hold onto the glimmer of hope,
That someday I'll find my way back to shore.

Is it alright if I silence the red-hot rage,
That simmers just beneath the surface?
The fiery anger threatens to erupt,
But I swallow it down, fearing its destructive force.

Is it well if I draw back from carrying the weight of
the world,
On my weary shoulders?
The burden feels heavy, like a leaden gray cloud,
But I'm afraid to let it go, afraid of what lies
beneath.

Is it fine to not be myself?
In the pale gray of conformity,
I lose sight of who I am,
Trying to fit into a mold that was never meant for me.

I tend to lose balance, teetering on the edge,
Caught between the black and white of right and wrong. But in the quiet moments of solitude,
I find solace in the soft brown earth beneath my feet, Grounding me, reminding me of my roots.

I find myself clueless about what to do in life,
Lost in a swirling whirlwind of uncertainty.
But in the warm brown of possibility,
I dare to dream, to imagine a future,
Where anything is possible, where I am enough.

Isn't it strange to dream and plan for a future,
When I know that reality may not align?
But in the technicolor tapestry of life,
I find beauty in the contrast,
In the juxtaposition of light and dark,
Of joy and sorrow, of hope and fear.

So, is it okay to not be okay?
In the mosaic of human experience,
I realize that it's not only okay,
But necessary to embrace the full spectrum of
emotions, To acknowledge the blues and the reds,
The grays and the blacks,
The whites and the browns,
And to find strength in the colorful chaos of
existence.

4. Unworthy

I mean besides my fault, which is the crossroad of
my unnoticed fate,
Like a picture, the handiwork of the untamed
graffiti artist,
In the setting of life, I have to slouch,
A black sheep among masterworks.

I am not like silkworm, making fabric from the
leaves, Nor am I as nimble and quick as an
antonym,
The container of my grades has sharp ends,
That are too astute to fail badly.

The wait for the unfinished things is heavy,
A cross I am bearing every day,
I spend many mornings and evenings, looking for
the exit in the daily maze,
My insecurities are getting the best of me.

I am told, "I want to make this hard for you so that
you remember that everything is not for everyone".

The image of perfection is an evil sun acting as a mirage, It is a luring shelter of comfort that abandons everybody,
The hollowness persists when we are starved of our souls.
Our identity is not of the flawless kind,
On the contrary, the cracks are the points from where the rays of light do enter,
Survivors of atrocities are not the ones who get the precious, glistering prize,
But those who are ready and brave to embark on their rocky and serene journey.

5. What Am I?

Hardwork and studies? Yes I do!
I study but when I do, they don't see
And later they make fun of me
Am I for that use?
When you are angry scold me, put me down, make me regret my existence and make me ask myself several questions
Am I like a plastic?
Use and then throw me away
Am I a stress ball?
Squeeze and twist me, mold my heart into another shape and coat it with a layer of fear like you coat the ball with black dirt
Am like a worn-out pencil?
Scribbling me away in the margins of life
Am I merely a tool, a disposable utensil?
Use me, abuse me, and toss me aside like yesterday's lunch wrapper

The questions, the taunts and the stares were yours, but the answers will be MINE!
And I am NOT going to be the shoes for your feet

~ Tales of the Inner Self ~

1. Heartstrings and Friendships

When the world slows down, just before the sun comes up, I often think about the people in my life. Family and friends – they're the ones who make everything better, who help us stand tall when we feel small.

Family is funny. They're not perfect, but they love us like no one else can. They've seen us grow up, from our first wobbly steps to our awkward teenage years. They're always there, cheering us on, and showing us how to be strong and true to ourselves. As a teenager, life can get pretty confusing. That's when I turned to my family. They're my safe place, always ready to listen and give me advice. Their words stuck with me, a reminder that I'm never really alone.

But life isn't just about family. It's also about friends – the ones who make us laugh and help us through tough times. We're all figuring out life together, sharing the good and the bad.
They always see the good in me, even when I can't. They believe in me, and that gives me the courage to chase my dreams, no matter what stands in my

way.
It's not just one friend, though. It's all my friends who keep me going. They're there to celebrate when I win and pick me up when I fall. They remind me that I can do amazing things, as long as they've got my back.

Thinking about all this, I feel thankful. My family and friends have shown me what love and friendship mean. They've taught me that I deserve to be loved, even when times are tough.

If you're reading this, remember to hold on to the people who care about you. Keep them close and never forget how much they mean to you. With their support, you can go after your dreams and be the best you can be.
And to my family and friends, I just want to say thank you. Thank you for being there for me, and for guiding me through the dark. Together, we're stronger than we could ever be on our own, tied together by love and friendship that'll last forever.
I would like to mention the initials of my closest friends- S.B, A.A, D.B, S.A, P.F, S.Y, T.A

Heartships forge the strongest friendships, like stars that shine brightest in the darkest nights, guiding us through life's journey.

2. Finding Love: A Journey Of The Heart

Love is like a soft summer wind or the gentle shine of the moon on a night when the sky is clear. It's something you can't hold or see, but it's always around. It's a warm feeling that starts deep inside you. A little spark that lifts your spirits and makes you feel good and happy.

I didn't always believe in love. I was careful and didn't want to get hurt, especially after seeing how love can sometimes lead to sadness. But then, when I wasn't looking for it, love came into my life out of nowhere.

I found love in the small things, not in big actions or fancy gifts. It was in a smile we shared, a hand to hold when I needed comfort, and kind words when I needed support. It was in the way they looked at me, making me feel like I was the most important person in the world, and in the way being with them made me feel complete.

Slowly, love started to become a part of my life. It fixed what was broken and made me feel whole in a way I never had before. It was like finding the piece I was missing, and now my life felt right.

But love isn't always simple. It needs patience, kindness, and the ability to forgive and make compromises. Sometimes the journey is tough and the future is not clear, but that's when love is the strongest. It lights up the dark and helps us keep going with hope.

Love has taught me to accept and care for others. It has shown me that it's okay to be open and that there's strength in letting go. Love has changed the way I see the world, making it kinder and more caring.

Looking back, I see that love is more than just a feeling – it's a way of living. It's about being kind and respectful to others and helping them up when they're down. Love connects us all, no matter where we are or when we are.

So, if you're reading this, I want to tell you to let love into your heart. It might not be easy, but it's worth it. Love can heal, inspire, and change us in ways we never imagined.

And to the one I love, know that you've changed my life in the best ways. You're my guide, my support, and the joy in my heart. With you, I believe we can do anything, because love wins over everything.

And there's something else about love, it's like a seed that grows. At first, it might not seem like much, just a tiny thing buried in the ground. But with a little care, it starts to grow. It pushes through the soil and reaches for the sun. That's how love is. It starts small, but it grows bigger and stronger over time, reaching out and touching everything around it.

Love also teaches us about ourselves. It's like holding up a mirror and seeing who we really are. Sometimes, it shows us the best parts of ourselves—the parts that are kind and brave. Other times, it shows us the parts that need a little work. But that's okay because love is patient. It waits for us to get better, to learn, and to grow. Love doesn't give up on us, even when we make mistakes.

Love ties us together with invisible strings, making life's dance a bit more magical.

3. My Part Of The World

A rising topic where most teens feel left out, maybe because they don't feel the affection they are getting or sometimes we tend to question ourselves. Well, we do that all the time infact without leaving any part of the night as an overthinker. This is an essential part!

In my part of the world, every day is a new story, a new lesson, a new opportunity to grow. And I wouldn't trade it for anything else.

In my part of the world I include the rikshaw bells ringing on the street, the delicious waterball stall [golgappa/puchka], the flickering street lights and those moment I spend in books, with my family and friends.

In my part of world the most important position is held by myself. Yes, you would also want to believe at this point that the most important person in your path is you yourself, but you don't want to, right? Because you degrade yourself most of the times, you demotivate yourself before even starting a project. But we all need to know that believing in ourselves is an important cup of tea that we have to pay as equal attention as we give to other priorities. Come on let us shout out to ourselves “YES WE CAN”.

In my part of world I include those fictional characters I read in books. Ones who have my heart and ones who have my soul. I am attached to them as if they are those personalities residing withing me.

In my part of world, those neighbors, helping and caring for us are highly valuable. Our chit chats and sharing things is like a daily habit, that can never be avoided.

In my part of world, I wake up with the bustling of the busy street early in the morning and the fresh aroma of chai and breakfast that somehow soothes my nerves

I don’t consider my part of world as a geographical structure but a living and breathing entity, where people breathe love and affection, they live for each other as well as for themselves. If others can, why can’t we? Ask this question to yourself and let your inner voice answer it.

I'm learning to balance tradition with modernity, responsibility with passion, and individuality with community. This is my part of the world, complex yet captivating, challenging yet full of promise.

In every part of the world, there's a rhythm that beats, a story that unfolds, and a beauty that's uniquely its own, waiting to be discovered and cherished.

4. I Can Do It

I CAN DO IT. One sentence, four words, and eight letters but the impact of these letters on us when we say it out loud is something undefinable, uncountable and it's a hundred times more meaningful when said to our own self. Yes, I am talking about your courage to speak these four words to yourself. Stand in front of a mirror and say it out loud before going for any challenge that you are nervous or tensed about, and observe the magic it does. Let me ask you, Can You Do It? Wait I couldn't hear your response! Would you mind repeating your answer again? And I am expecting a big yes from all of you, say "Yes, I can do it". I am waiting.

Yes! That's the spirit. See you did it. Your first step towards believing in yourself self was to accept that you are capable of doing anything and everything that a person has or can have power over.

A few days back I was alone on this road of self-belief. Being a teenager, I know it's hard to do so. Self-doubt and questions charging us our sleep are always big boulders in this pathway, and that is what we need to overcome. Those big and heavy rocks are the ones we need to push away, clearing the road so that we can easily walk through it and reach the destination quickly.

Messages on self-upliftment worked as peaceful music, soothing my heart and bringing my soul to rest on the bed of my body for a while. [On this topic I indeed have to state my special gratitude to my parents, close friends, and myself.]

Removing these boulders from the way isn't a task of breaking a fifteen-foot-tall wall, yet it is a challenge that we must complete at any cost.

Start slowly but effectively. If we add a hundred coins of one rupee/dollar each, it will add up to a hundred rupees/dollars, now if we go back we can observe that one rupee couldn't get you a lot but once you've saved all of those one rupee coins it does have a value. The same goes for us, one step at a time, a small initiative, for example, start by completing one task a day, it can be work turned in to you by your academic coach or maybe a goal you've set up for yourself. I am sure on that hundredth day, you are going to applaud yourself for keeping patience and using it as a key to your success. This is not a success which awards you a gold or silver medal but it is the one where you win yourself.

"I CAN DO IT" is not just a phrase, it's a powerful declaration of self-belief, a mantra that fuels the spirit to overcome any obstacle with determination and grit.

5. The Unseen Chapters

Academics, for a teenager like me, isn't just about the grades or the subjects, it's a rollercoaster of emotions, a journey of self-discovery amidst the pages of textbooks and the scribbles in notebooks. It's the nervous butterflies before a test, the warmth of pride from a teacher's praise, and sometimes, the sting of a disappointing mark.

Every day, I juggle equations, essays, and experiments, each one a stepping stone towards my future. But these aren't just academic exercises, they're life lessons in disguise. They teach me patience when a concept doesn't click in my mind, resilience when I fail, and joy in the small victories when I succeed.

The classroom is my second home, where I'm not just a student, but a dreamer, a thinker, a friend. It's where I've shared secret glances and silent giggles with my classmates, where we've all sighed in unison at the announcement of a pop quiz. It's where I've seen my peers struggle and shine, reminding me that we're all in this together.

But it's not always easy. There are days when the weight of expectations feels too heavy, when the balance between school and life tips has shaken, and I find myself lost in a sea of 'shoulds' and 'musts'. It's in these moments that I learn the most about myself, about my limits, my strengths, and my ability to push through.

And then there's life outside the classroom, where I'm more than just a student. I'm a sibling, sharing laughs over dinner, a friend trading stories under the stars, a teenager navigating the complexities of growing up. These roles may seem separate from academics, but they're inter-connected, each one influencing the other, shaping the person I am becoming.

As I stand on the brick of adulthood, I realize that academics is more than just knowledge, it's a journey of the heart as well as the mind. It's about finding passion in the pages of a book, forming friendships over a shared problem set, and learning not just from textbooks, but from every experience life throws my way.

In the grand tapestry of life, my academic journey is just one thread, but it's a foundational one. It shapes my work ethic, my curiosity, and my understanding of the world. And as much as I might grumble about homework or stress about exams, I know that this journey is shaping me into the person I'm meant to become.

Sometimes, academics feels like a puzzle where each piece is a different class or assignment. I find myself trying to fit everything together, making sense of the bigger picture. It's like every day is a new challenge, a new opportunity to learn something that might just be the key to solving the puzzle of my future.

But it's not just about the future. It's about the here and now, the daily grind of getting up for school, sitting through lessons, and doing homework. It's about the friendships formed over shared notes and the inside jokes that only we understand. It's about the teachers who inspire us and the ones who challenge us to do better.

Then there's the part of academics that nobody sees, the late night studies, the stress, the worry about not being good enough. It's the silent battles we fight with ourselves, the constant questioning of whether we're on the right path. But it's also the personal victories, the moments when we overcome our doubts and prove to ourselves that we can do it.

And let's not forget the life lessons that come disguised as algebra problems and essay prompts. They teach us more than just the subject matter, they teach us about life. They show us how to deal with failure, how to celebrate success, and how to keep pushing forward no matter what.

So, here I am, a teenager navigating the maze of academics, trying to find the balance between doing well in school and enjoying my youth. It's a tricky balance, but it's my balance to find. And as I grow and learn, I carry with me the lessons from both my successes and my failures, knowing that each step, each stumble, is a part of my story, a story that's still being written.

Every teen's academic journey has an unseen chapter, filled with silent struggles and quiet victories, shaping the story that the world seldom reads.

6. Life's Unexpected Journey

Life is a journey full of unexpected turns and twists, much like a winding river that flows through the vast landscape of time. It's unpredictable, exciting, and sometimes a bit scary. As a teenager, I've come to realize that life doesn't always follow the neat, straight paths we lay out in our minds. It's more like a game of snakes and ladders, where one roll of the dice can send you climbing up high or sliding down low.

When I was younger, I thought I had it all figured out. I had plans for everything: what I'd study, where I'd go to college, and even the kind of people I'd hang out with. But life, with its playful smirk, had other ideas set for me. It threw curveballs that I never saw coming towards me. Friends moved away, interests changed, and the subjects I thought I'd love turned out to be as dull as a rainy day with muddy ground and the cloud all black, just like the dull moment of life I was living at that particular moment.

The twists and turns of life have taught me to be flexible. Like a tree that bends in the wind but doesn't break similar to a banana tree. I've learned to adapt to change. I've discovered strengths I didn't know I had and faced fears I never thought I could conquer. I've learned that sometimes, taking a detour can lead to the most beautiful views.

Life's unpredictability has also taught me to appreciate the moment. We often get so caught up in planning for the future that we forget to enjoy the present and the present slips off our hand turning into past. But the truth is, we don't know what tomorrow holds. So, I've learned to savor the laughter, the late-night talks, and even the simple joy of a sunny day.

As I stand here, a teenager so lost, I realize that life's unknown turns and twists aren't something to fear. They're what make life thrilling. They're the stories we'll one day cherish and let it out to the upcoming generations or maybe to our little siblings. These are going to be the memories we'll look back on with a smile. So, I say, bring on the adventure. Let the river of life take me where it will. I'm ready for the ride.

Take my life, for example. I planned to join the basketball team, but I ended up in the drama club instead. It was unexpected, but it turned out to be one of the best things ever. I made new friends and discovered a passion for acting. It was a twist I didn't see coming, but I'm glad it happened.

These twists teach us to be flexible. When life throws a curveball, we learn to catch it or dodge it. We learn that it's okay to change direction and try new things. And sometimes, these changes lead to amazing adventures we never imagined.

So, embrace life's twists and turns. They might be scary, but they can also lead to great things. Just go with the flow and enjoy the ride. That's what makes life exciting – not knowing what's next but facing it head-on anyway.
Life, with all its unknown turns and twists, is a beautiful mess. It's a tapestry woven with threads of experiences, some bright and vibrant, others dark and challenging. But together, they create a picture that's uniquely ours. As I continue to navigate through this maze called life, I do so with an open heart and an eager spirit, ready to embrace whatever comes my way. After all, it's these very twists and turns that make life such an incredible adventure.

In the end, life's twists and turns are what shape us. They're the chapters in our story that make us who we are. And as I write this, as a teenager still figuring it all out, I'm excited to see where my path will lead. Maybe it won't be where I planned, but that's just fine. Because in life, the beauty often lies in the journey, not the destination.

Leaving a few pages empty for you and for me to write and annotate the words we feel are true for ourselves in the upcoming hour, day, month, or year.
I want this anthology to be a part that we feel is our own.

Thank you to all the readers, for patiently turning one page after another and completing this whole series of self-discovery.

Teenage years are the pages where the ink of life spills most freely, crafting a story of unexpected turns and twists that shape the chapters to come.

Sometimes, the best thing we can do is turn the page, start a new chapter, and just keep writing our story. Let's move on, not because the past isn't important, but because our future has so much more to offer.

Let's cherish the ending as much as the beginning, because every ending is just a new start in disguise.

In the canvas of existence, every human stroke paints a story.

Embrace life's dance, where each step reveals a universe of possibilities.

Life's journey is a stream, simple yet profound, where each moment is a reflection of our shared humanity. In its flow, we find the essence of existence, as every experience weaves into the tapestry of time. Embrace the simplicity, for it holds life's deepest truths.

www.ingramcontent.com/pod-product-compliance
Lightning Source LLC
La Vergne TN
LVHW091320150826
845673LV00006B/1706
* 9 7 8 9 3 6 0 8 3 1 9 9 8 *